The Wars That Steer Us

The Wars That Steer Us

Reverie Koniecki

Grateful acknowledgments to the following:
"Clarence Thomas Plays With My Pussy" *Rigorous Magazine*
"That year, we burned" *Rigorous Magazine*

The Wars That Steer Us

Mouthfeel Press is an indie press publishing works in English and Spanish by new and established poets. We publish poetry, fiction, and non-fiction. Our print books are available through our independent bookstores, website, Bookshop.org, and other online and independent booksellers, or at author's readings. Ebooks are available through KOBO.

Cover Art by Octavio Quintanilla
Art Title: Frontextos, Nepantlarte 53
Cover Design: Karen Dreher

Contact Information:

Mouthfeelbooks.com
Info.mouthfeelbooks@gmail.com

Print ISBN: 978-1-957840-15-4
Ebook ISBN: 978-1-957840-16-1

Published in the United States, 2023
First Printing in English
$12

Table of Contents

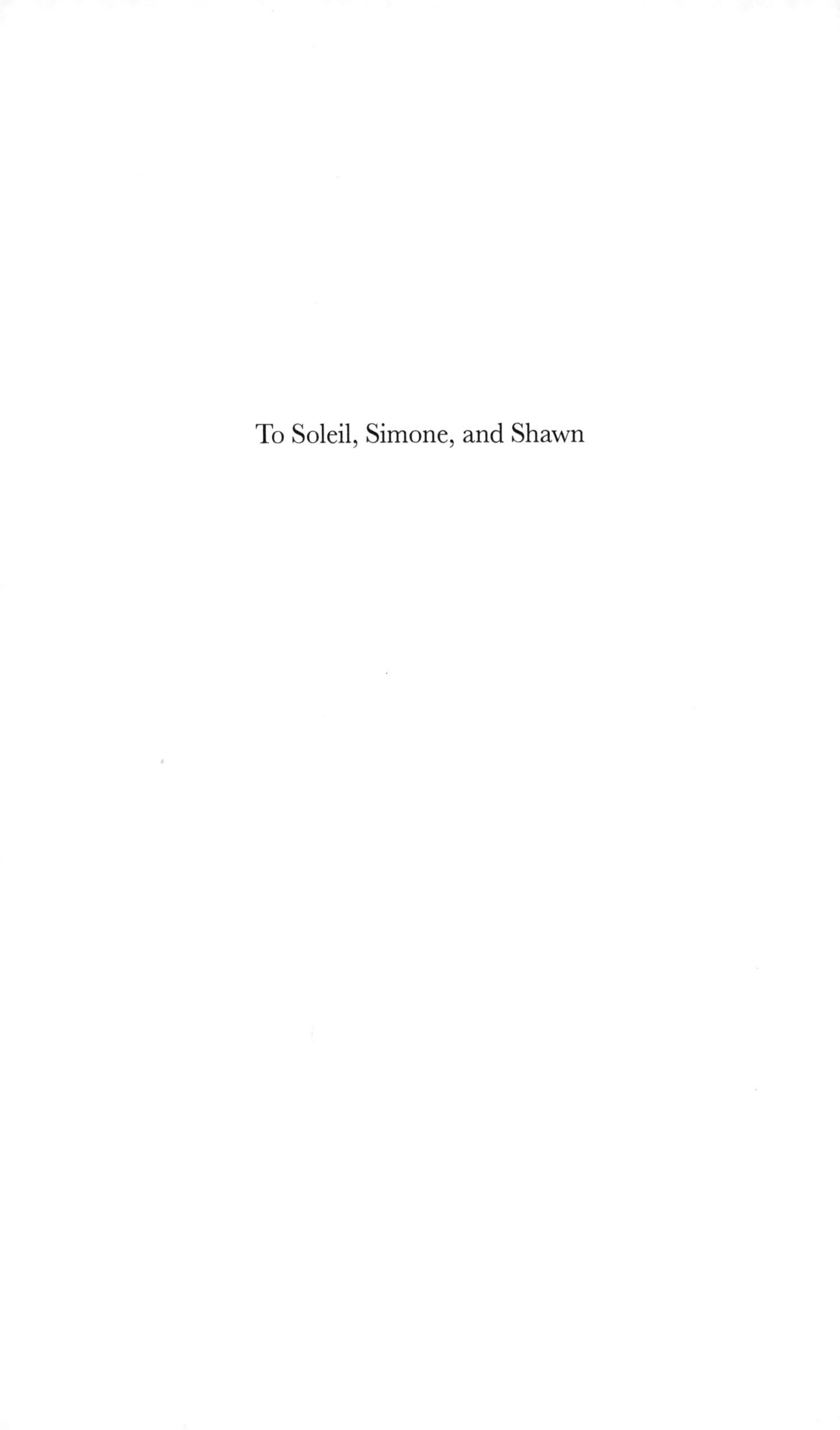

To Soleil, Simone, and Shawn

The Wars That Steer Us

the wars that steer us

I sit on the wicker hamper outside
the bathroom barely able to stay quiet
pre-adolescent girl giggles
carbonate my throat
you emerge escorted by shower fog
the scent of dove soap and jergens
wearing a clean face and nightgown
pink foam rollers line your hair
uniformly like headstones

I execute my joke and
roar with all my stomach
into the small night of the hallway
your hands move efficiently knotting
themselves around my neck
hair follicles on my arms rise
heads coming out of prayer
tulips breaking ground
in the last leg of winter
jesus on the third day
I quickly understand that jokes
are battlefields of undeclared wars

the currency of the spleen has no value here
no matter how many metaphors you throw
at a rock, it will always be a rock
which is to say you wished
my father loved you enough to stay
my father half man all beast
with whom I share this uncivilized language
there are no pictures of him
there is only me
perched on the coffee table
with the smile of a minotaur
it is as if we were never here

I'm all you've got you'd say
with the remorse and pain
of a chipped tooth
the smell of my blue magic coated
cornrows breaks the spell
you realize I am not
the monster you seek
this is not a fucking game
you say quietly
voice omnipresent
the hum of the refrigerator
controlled with threat
anyone would sacrifice
the small animal of themselves
for love if they had to

to save her dying country

skin too taboo
to talk about in a classroom

a narrative labeled
as dangerous and

divisive
community backlash

against books
about rosa parks

this revised pathology
this remembering

this crime that unifies us
i feel blacker against

a white backdrop
a subordinate gold rush

we are panning
for coal for flowers for

give me a fucking break
nigger eyes?

the first black _________
to be legally black

opponents have
the right to bear arms

a coat of arms
in Mississippi the children

eat blood
heartbeats are weaponized

as a uterus writhes
grinding what teeth cannot

a flag incites our deepest riot
we imagine our deaths

airplanes and cumulus clouds
this is the closest we will get

to heaven
it's something in the eyes

press the gas for the ending
we feel the needle cross

the threshold of skin deep
we don't want it but will beg

for it later the way
the oppressed thirst

to defile their mistresses
windchimes warn of wind

there are always more bodies
to crucify for posthumous

admissions of guilt
the taste of salt

before emptying one's stomach
the crimson that refills it

it was always about the bloodshed
and the breast it leaks from

we have conquered

my grandmother chewed snuff
and kept a tin cup by her bed
for the tar she gathered on her gums

hustling up quarters for milk
she still believes in a day
when dining room tables
will overflow with fruit

and children play in mouths of lions
after her man left she wept
after my mother gave up bacon she wept

I step inside her rib cage
extend my arms through the sleeves
I want to love myself

as much as she does
a ferris wheel keeps time
with every ticking revolution

our questions remain ignored
like unfamiliar area codes
we collect the ears

of enemies we have conquered
and hang their bowels
on the windows like garland

warding off malevolent spirits
we break bread until
our poverty is quieted

we were born with barbed wire
mufflers eaten by rust
a cough away from losing

their tailpipes hanging on like
the lover you no longer desire
I crawl out of this gutted body

and fall into the loneliness
of my mother's dry-aged breast
an ochre velvet winged moth

forgets how to fly
its dull knife motion makes me
believe it is making progress

it was always about the bloodshed
and the breast it leaks from

the visit

any stranger can be your priest
you run with hands in pockets
to answer the doorbell
on the other side of the window
a sunflower bobs it's golden crown
and charred face
there is no wind today
you are not expecting visitors but
you let the animals in anyway
they come marching in packs
they come chanting like protesters
imagining a world of inclusion
they come bearing frankincense and myrrh
they come up the front stoop
leaving tracks on my freshly
mopped kitchen floor.
they set up in the living room
bears sit on the couch
causing it to sag and creak in the middle
sparrows perch on my mantle
an orchestra of languages fill the room
on the floor is shoulder to shoulder chaos
pairs of snakes
beavers with paddles
raccoons with sleepless glinting eyes
the ostrich stomps her feet
accidentally kicking one of the cockatoos
who lets out the scream
of a mother crowning a 10 lb baby
wolves howl and lunge
for deer who scuttle
upstairs and lock
themselves in my bedroom
they are terrified the way
black people fear the police
the wolves bear teeth

instead of badges and guns
you trip over a turtle as you
race up behind them
the animals follow you
filling the narrow hallway
a rabbit shits in the corner
everyone is screaming now
glass chimes like a fallen soldier
who fought for someone else's beliefs
you open the door in time
to see tufts of whiteness
disappear over the ledge

White Girl

i was the blackest thing
my classmates had ever seen

they'd chant *brownie, brownie*
as i walked home from school

i don't remember the first time
they called me a nigger

my cousins called me nature girl
because I went barefoot and

climbed the same willow trees
that we picked our switches from

it was more proof
that I was the white girl

they accused me of being.
i was guilty of not living in the city

not knowing how to play double dutch
or navigate myself to the corner store

my aunt once stroked my ashy
arms and told her neighbor

this is my white niece
i don't know why my sister

brought them kids out there
to live with them white folks

listen to them talk she said
exposing my constructions

vowels obeying hardened consonants
and curtsying before the next word.

segregated from my mother tongue
i lick my dry blackness

to reconstitute adhesion
in this space of not belonging.

the runner

for Amhaud Arbery

your slow simmering skin
the tone of your stretched
muscles and ligaments
feet slapping the road
granules of sweat
dripping from both hemispheres
somewhere a heron takes flight from a bridge
it's outline disappears in the horizon
like the line between body and memory
you are free

the tone of your stretched
feet slapping the road
muscles and ligaments
your heart revolts against your ribs
this is the longest race
there is no finishing line or medal
no time to call for your mother
no sins left to repent

the hunters are as ruthless as
the second amendment
feet slapping the road
feet slapping the road
feet slapping the road
stretched muscles and
ligaments burning
they take aim
you wonder if your mother
will feel this before she knows
feet slapping the road
then arms chest and head
you discover the difference
between flying and failing
is assonance

Red

1. Connected by a single letter, we endure silence the way nonbelievers learn to swim.

2. The pulp of a tooth turns black when its predators are unknown.

3. Hospitals are at full capacity and Tucker Carlson continues to rant.

4. Greg Abbott is an idiot.

5. The weight of a man. A husband tells his wife that she chooses to be that way after she says she is falling apart. As if windshields choose to shatter.

6. Bread molds after seven days. The half-life of a biscuit is enough to summon a flood of spores. I am airborne.

7. I have picked switches for sins for which I can not be absolved.

8. American History: *Let's talk about slavery and see who disappears first.*

9. l am burning hydrogen. Generations intersect my skin.

10. It's meet-the-teacher night and the parents want to know if I will teach Critical Race Theory. I tell them that my mother willed me her body. Nail polish chipped. Fingers calloused. Toes cracked.

11. My grandmother puts me to work in the fields. We pick sugarcane side by side, working mechanically. Her hands are soft as wet paper.

the blackest summer/

hashtags/
everyone dying
for some reason or another
until a virus becomes as benign
as eating brussel sprouts and ham for dinner/
we cocooned into roadkill
slumbering in break down lanes
all fur and claws/
joints angled at injustice/
drawing eyes to a fixed point
a single stain
a single black dot
this is not my heritage
the night howls thickly/
sidewalks are so hot
there is no handshake/
you–caught between bicep and forearm/
a chokehold is the first dance
in this marriage between nation and body/
a union predicated on skin
not made for breaking/
in the morning all of your shards are intact
like the moments before your lover leaves/
you shower, dress, make coffee,
expect the privilege of sameness/
but the latest video
of a black man dying on a sidewalk/
but the latest rising numbers of the pandemic/
but a president who doesn't care/
you finish your coffee/
you call your mother who expresses her wish
to be left alone with 45 in the oval office for just a few minutes/
your friends text you and ask if you are okay/
you tell them everyone is dying
for some reason or another

Clarence Thomas Plays With My Pussy

a woman asks for change at the bus stop
I give her a boxcutter and a turkey leg
she bleeds
clots rush down her legs like funeral tears
I understand that she is saying thank you
I didn't know it would hurt this much, she says
I tell her my grandmother disappeared
in a swarm of mosquitoes
all that was left of her body
was the handle of her machete
and the jungle
the sound is deafening
why am I always naked
if you want to know the truth
interrogate my snatch
with your biggest speculum
light a match
tell me what you see
press me hard against
your examination table
spatchcock my sternum
stretch my legs into stirrups
my nipple hard and black
as the pipeline to prison
you offer me food stamps
and powdered milk
If the shoe fits, you say
a cat can have kittens in an oven
but I wouldn't call them biscuits, I reply
you set the thermostat to broiling
I believe you are the alpha and omega
how else can you explain
the balled up fast food wrappers
the newports,
carter bloodcare,
my blood splashing on the black

and white checkered linoleum
like piss on a sidewalk
I shiver and ask for a napkin
fold the corners into neat triangles
did you know you can only fold paper
so many times before it refuses to bend over

That year, we burned.

We sit in front of the television offering alms, palms skyward, knees kissing the freshly baptized hardwood. Our bodies are as clean as innocence, but we have already seen. On screen, the governor stands in front of the courthouse as the neighborhood burns, offering thoughts and prayers. There is not an unclenched tooth in the crowd that encircles him like a morning fog. They demand a body. Any black body. "No one is going to die tonight," the governor says, just before a bullet inseminates the chambers of his heart like a growing fetus.

Everything hinges on a lie. A screen door slams itself shut as the mosquitoes search for blood in the night. The war zone is a library. Books snatched by their spines, taken hostage under the guise of preserving history. Their mouths duct taped shut before being tossed into the fire. What about the children, someone asks. What about the children, someone responds.

From ashes our ancestors rise and remind us that silence will not protect us. My grandfather says the earth will be cleansed and nods his head in revelation. He tells me to remember the water and takes a deep drag from his Pall Mall. He is an indignant stain on a white shirt, bleached in the name of Forgetting.

twice as hard

we are hanging our laundry
my mother works rhythmically

pinning our undergarments to the line
the parched gray city, stoic behind her

*one time I fought back
I hit your father so hard*

I might have broken his jaw
she says matter of factly

her words flow easily like music
as easily as first time a man's

knuckles hardened around my neck
a paper crane takes flight

over her sun-crowned head
and I feel less alone

I wonder if I deserve it
our sheets are lonely ghosts

billowing boneless bodies
clothespins spread apart like buoys

markers defining the threadbare line
between enough and drowning

the recidivist wife

The hornet's hips bell out
as shamelessly as his mistress
The metallic whine of its pointed wings,
the swift thud of a butcher's blade
cutting through bone.
An inhale slices her throat.
Her dream diffuses
leaving behind the scent
of an argument.

She has awakened in a desert
of small appliances.
She never wanted pots and pans
or dish towels or ladles.
The aloe vera on the counter
sheds her outer arms
like that Christmas
she left with nothing.
Her desires are inaudible
to the weight of a scale.

She doesn't recognize
the knobbed knuckles
the raised veins.
She knocks.
Again.

She remembers the leaves,
slick against the street.
The moist hiss of tires.
Misted rain beading her hair.
Before he opened.
Those shallow breathing seconds.
Bones of light and ash are behind her.

Sweat drips down her spine like morphine.
She wishes.
It was like coming home.
He was home.

She picks bluebonnets
knowing they will die.
The pasture rolls back its neck
and asks for a kiss.
Crouching in this grass
tall enough to hide regrets,
she waits.

ancestors

when you kiss the sun
it becomes an accomplice
to extinction
a shadow casting light
despite burnt offerings
the earth drowns

there is no ark where
you are welcome
you must know
your value in water
because stories go down
easier than promises
with no acres nor mule
you live on the edge
severed umbilically
from two continents
straddling the water
always the water

at the bottom
of this passage
are bodies to tabulate
bodies to tabulate
bodies to tabulate
liabilities before being

tossed overboard

for indemnification

yet water doesn't cleanse

anymore than eloquence

good manners and

muscles are of no consequence

your body has no answers

your gods have no answers

wails fill the air like milk

in a suckling baby's stomach

the slap of salt on skin

the first of many lashings

history in medias

tell the children to remember

the bodies the bodies the bodies

Lot's Wife

I have a name
despite his wrath

god's messengers glistened
like post coital thighs arms

breasts entangled subject
object in any order out of order

there is no desire without shame
I shed my leaves in that wide arc

between hunger and flesh
they were so lividly gorgeous

you couldn't help but want
give us this day our daily bread

I tell my daughters nothing is clean
when your name is blotted out

an offensive stain on a page
the only voice that matters is your husband's

when he made an offering of my daughters
to the men who wanted to defile angels

I bowed like an hungover daisy
and whispered his name

for thine is the power
so when the city fell

I turned back

the language you should understand

*for your mother who went to every school
board meeting to make space for your body*

your mother tries to kiss you
and incises your cheek instead
you don't speak for light years
until the injury is so far away
it doesn't matter anymore
there is no apology
only the weariness of anger
yet you make revolutions
ruminating the block as many times
as you can fit into a lunch hour
this is the season you will
go the wrong way on a one way
you complain about your mother
to anyone with a nodding head
you run as far as your smoker's
lungs will take you
mapquesting 1700 miles
across country with 50
bucks in your bank account
baby strapped to your back
you flee a cold unfriendly city
to another cold unfriendly city
with the tools of complacency
stowed in the trunk of your car
bone, sharp teeth, monogamy
you are as naive as the uniformed
children plunging into the crosswalk
electrophiles from third marriages
predictable plaids and knee socks
conjugating hot chips and kool-aid pickles
fingers caked with the subtitled

language of salted red pollen
and saliva streaking thighs
destinies illuminated in taillights
of dissipating traffic
you brand yourself a new name
with the earnestness of revelation
you, connoisseur of Ted Talks
you, unsuspecting mother tongue
you, bearer of out-of-wedlock children
bending to raised eyebrows
like a willow branch
not everyone believes in the river
but everyone is immersed
in a god that will eventually kill them
under the cinch of the Bible Belt
you become fluent
in the language of the city
squat trees with sparse shadows
burning grass at the side of the highway
scalding upholstery that sticks to your thighs
air as unforgiving as a pair of jeans
one size too small
you forgive your mother and
start to see her as a woman
strings of grackle lining a stoplight
swarm into choreograph
rising and falling like the stock market
black waves collapsing into small
undeveloped countries

the night is

rittenhouse got off and a nation
inside of a nation rejoices the way
a fetus sometimes kills its mother
I don't search for answers for the same
reason I don't search for my father

this is our offspring
the muscle memory of a promise
the full moon of an argument
a family secret sealed in a ziplock
the drunk uncle
passed out in front of the liquor store

the highway slices the neighborhood
it is a clean severing of joints
blood irrigates the corner store
where newports and swisher sweets
wait to be plucked from trees
herringbones are mined from concrete
potholes break the spines of cars
children salivate over scratch
and sniff stickers

it is easy to bear witness when
your loyalty has never been tested
on the other side of the block
slow cooked meat falls apart at the
slightest provocation of the fork
in protest of being captured whole

we kneel like sinners at bedtime
do boolean searches for mercy
my dead grandmother has no birth certificate
her legacy—palmolive hands

and baby powder
it's in the Bible she assures me
every hair on your head is numbered
I try to count

Orion shines nakedly in the sky
we pray to the money blessing tree
to fill the cracks in the sidewalk
while burning incense and weed for the gods
the old lady at the smoke shop calls me baby
her black lips are a lunar eclipse
the bell jingles as I exit
I pack myself into a stray grocery cart
and push

Her Best Behavior

Dandelions have poisons dedicated
to eradicating their existence
because it's impolite to dream
on a yard someone else has claimed.
My mother has taken root in me and bloomed.
She is a birthday candle dancing
fluidly despite the assault of breath.
Embers of her body diffuse
like talcum powder on my
grandmother's body after a bath.
This is the offense.
To be everywhere and nowhere.
The mouth is a common executioner.
I've been resurrected from many last words.
I'm no Lady Lazarus, but
I'm the kind of woman who says things like
—*god I hate insurance*, and
I'll have half a pound of the Lebanese bologna,
and *yes ma'am I'll talk to him*
about those missing assignments.
I live in a cemetery of small appliances.
My headstone reads—
this air fryer has a half-life left.
Preheat and my skin peels off in sheets
until I am nakedly standing
mid-street, not stopping traffic.
I am gloriously alive.
My daughters wear wigs and three inch eyelashes
that they flutter coquettishly like high beams issuing
a warning behind a driver who has forgotten
to turn on their head lamps.
I mourn the bubble gum pink of their childhoods each
time I pass a playground because this is
how I will always remember them.

I tell them to move like felines crouched in a bush.
That my voice will rise up within them
in their blackest moments.
I tell them to dig their own canals,
to machete their way across this continent
until their hands crack.

when you can't conquer the mountain

you keep going

knowing this shit will kill you

carrying your worn leather boots in your arms

the way you might cradle a fallen child

you disturb the earth as you dance

because resistance is another appetite

at the end of the horizon where

the sun melts like adolescence into nostalgia

you don't so much forgive as you forget

the violence

you were born with

eyes in the back of your head—

all of which are black

holes bending light

ingesting small galaxies

the universe has a tongue

that extracts itself from equations

after the loss of argument

listen to the silence hovering

like a dog under a table

begging to be broken

strong woman

she is a marble statue in the eye of the hurricane
alive, refusing to shudder down

or bend or snap or fly
despite the pleading of wind-whipped conifers.

she dances a rhythmless two-step when it rains
because it reminds her of childhood

her chiseled breasts, unplucked
fruit dangling from the vine

long past ripening or desire
suede skin, not supple, but softened by time

an emergency C-section scar divides
her torso into mirrored images

endlessly reverberating what has been lost
forget about her pain

tell her she is strong
for the meek shall inherit the earth

tell her to be silent
for her silence will protect her

love her
for thine is the image of a god

see her
walk the street wearing sensible shoes

booty shorts and a halter
her thighs rub together

a small balcony of back-fat spills over her bra
she wears painted-on eyebrows

sings lullabies to your niece
picks bluebonnets every April

she is first in line at the corner store
buying a pack of black and milds

she is never hungry
because strong women don't need

rain or allergies or pillows
to cover their tears

you can pierce her skin
and she wouldn't even bleed

rather her face glows as if illuminated
by headlamps seconds before collision

Author's Biography

Reverie Koniecki is a Black writer and educator living in Dallas, Texas. She earned her MFA in Poetry and Creative Nonfiction from New England College. Her work has appeared in *Guernica*, *HeavyFeather Review*, *Post Road*, *Rigorous Magazine* and other places. Her chapbook, *to the god of sore feet*, from Finishing Line Press was published in 2023.

Notes

In "to save her dying country," the line "nigger eyes" refers to Sylvia Plath's *Ariel*.

34

www.ingramcontent.com/pod-product-compliance
Lightning Source LLC
Chambersburg PA
CBHW040547170726
48295CB00012B/621